LIVING THINGS
and
A Compare and Contrast Book
NONLIVING THINGS

by Kevin Kurtz

Everywhere you go,
you will see
living things.

Everywhere you go,
you will see

nonliving things.

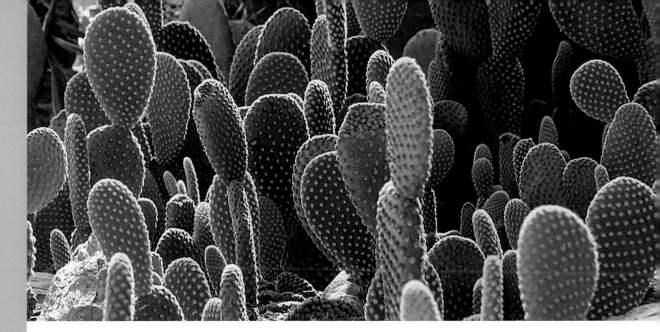

Living things

How are they
different from
each other?

Are living things
the only things
that move?

Not necessarily.
Some nonliving things move . . .

. . . while some living things cannot.

Are living things the only things that grow and change?

All living things do
grow and change.

But some nonliving things
grow and change too.

Are living things the only things that reproduce?

Do only living things make babies?

Or seeds?

Or copies of themselves?

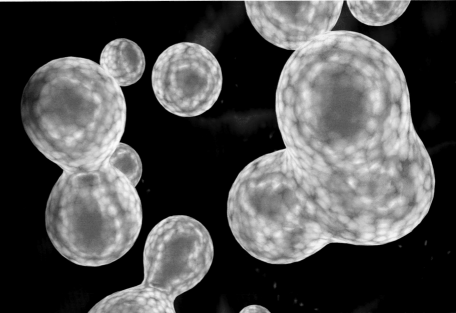

Some nonliving things can also make copies of themselves.

And though almost all living things can reproduce . . .

. . . some living things, like mules and male ligers, cannot.

Are living things the only things that need food?

That need water and breathe oxygen?

All living things do need energy, nutrients, and water to exist. Many of them also need to breathe oxygen to exist.

But, this nonliving thing also needs "food" and oxygen to exist.

This nonliving thing cannot exist without always getting water from its environment.

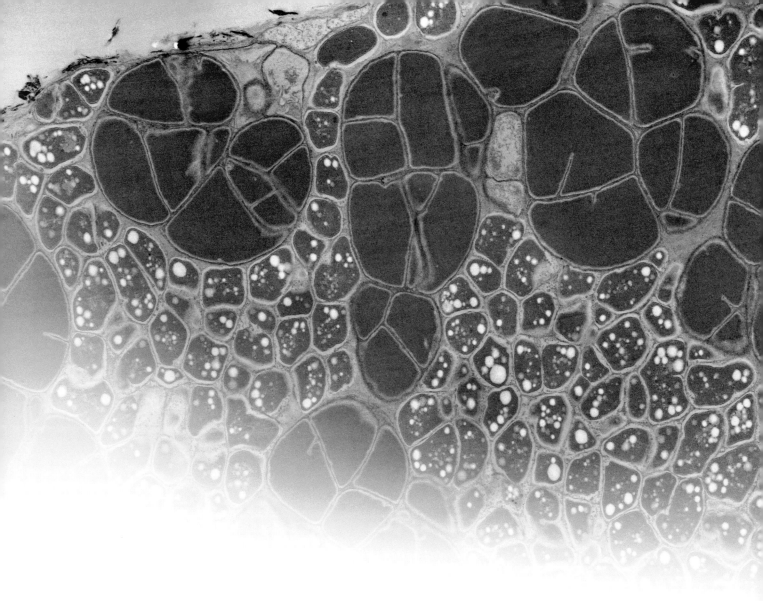

And some living things, like these microbes, are poisoned by oxygen. They breathe other things, like sulphur and even iron.

So how are living things
different from nonliving things?

Not even scientists have a
perfect answer.

But if something does ALL these things, then it is probably a living thing.

Breathe.

Drink Water.

Take energy and nutrients from its environment.

Reproduce.

Grow and change.

For Creative Minds

Glossary

Breathe: to take in and push out a gas

Energy: the ability to do work. Work can be anything something does, like move, think, grow, or reproduce.

Environment: a system made of living and nonliving things

Grow: to change, develop, or get bigger

Reproduce: to make a copy or a new thing like itself

What are some living things in your environment? Nonliving things?

People take in gas from their environment. They take in oxygen and push out carbon dioxide.

Plants take in gas from their environment. They take in carbon dioxide and push out oxygen.

What do you do that takes energy? How do you get energy from things in your environment?

Some nonliving things are not yet living things, or used to be living things but aren't any more. Which of the following was or will be a living thing?

- a mummy
- a marble statue
- frog eggs
- a painting of a person
- dinosaur bones
- a video of a cat
- petrified wood

If you make a drawing of a person, is that reproduction?

Answers: Was or will be a living thing: a mummy, frog eggs, dinosaur bones, petrified wood. Never a living thing: a marble statue, a painting of a person, a video of a cat

Living or Nonliving Checklist

Do you think this thing is living or nonliving? A living thing will meet most or all of the criteria on this checklist. For a printable version of this checklist, see the Teaching Activities at www.ArbordalePublishing.com.

bear

- ✔ Breathes
- ✔ Takes in water
- ✔ Gets nutrients and energy from its environment
- ✔ Reproduces
- ✔ Grows and changes

giraffe

- ? Breathes
- ? Takes in water
- ? Gets nutrients and energy from its environment
- ? Reproduces
- ? Grows and changes

- ? Breathes
- ? Takes in water
- ? Gets nutrients and energy from its environment
- ? Reproduces
- ? Grows and changes

penguin

Living: bear, penguin, giraffe. Nonliving: none

robot

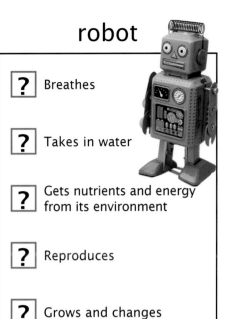

- **?** Breathes
- **?** Takes in water
- **?** Gets nutrients and energy from its environment
- **?** Reproduces
- **?** Grows and changes

airplane

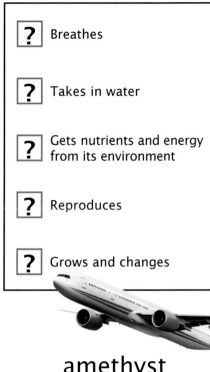

- **?** Breathes
- **?** Takes in water
- **?** Gets nutrients and energy from its environment
- **?** Reproduces
- **?** Grows and changes

frog

- **?** Breathes
- **?** Takes in water
- **?** Gets nutrients and energy from its environment
- **?** Reproduces
- **?** Grows and changes

train

- **?** Breathes
- **?** Takes in water
- **?** Gets nutrients and energy from its environment
- **?** Reproduces
- **?** Grows and changes

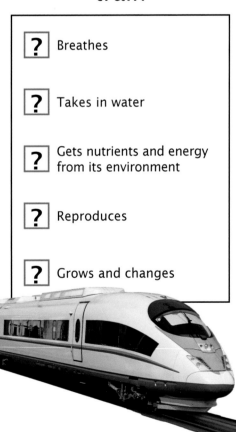

amethyst

- **?** Breathes
- **?** Takes in water
- **?** Gets nutrients and energy from its environment
- **?** Reproduces
- **?** Grows and changes

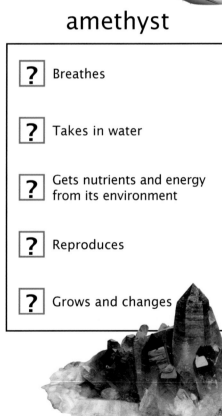

water

- **?** Breathes
- **?** Takes in water
- **?** Gets nutrients and energy from its environment
- **?** Reproduces
- **?** Grows and changes

Living: frog. Nonliving: robot, airplane, train, water, amethyst

ladybug

- **?** Breathes
- **?** Takes in water
- **?** Gets nutrients and energy from its environment
- **?** Reproduces
- **?** Grows and changes

fire

- **?** Breathes
- **?** Takes in water
- **?** Gets nutrients and energy from its environment
- **?** Reproduces
- **?** Grows and changes

teddy bear

- **?** Breathes
- **?** Takes in water
- **?** Gets nutrients and energy from its environment
- **?** Reproduces
- **?** Grows and changes

sea turtle

- **?** Breathes
- **?** Takes in water
- **?** Gets nutrients and energy from its environment
- **?** Reproduces
- **?** Grows and changes

sunflower

- **?** Breathes
- **?** Takes in water
- **?** Gets nutrients and energy from its environment
- **?** Reproduces
- **?** Grows and changes

volcano

- **?** Breathes
- **?** Takes in water
- **?** Gets nutrients and energy from its environment
- **?** Reproduces
- **?** Grows and changes

Living: ladybug, sunflower, sea turtle. Nonliving: fire, teddy bear, volcano

Graphic design by Mark Lawrence, using photos licensed through iStockPhoto or credited below. Shutterstock images used: Eric Isselee/55397161, Anton_Ivanov/154181657, g_tech/181037744, charles taylor/9977107, Aleksey Stemmer/151616837, ssuaphotos/105033176, Sailorr/172581671, CK Foto/462248086, Albert Russ/322450673, Potapov Alexander/126041540, irin-k/99075371, Marco Govel/124196191, Andrey tiyk/398822587, Peter Leahy/67266463, and Taku/422970898.

Thanks to Victoria Orphan (Caltech) and Tom Deerinck (NCMIR) for use of their anaerobic microbes photo.

Thanks to Lennie Dusek, Early Childhood Specialist at the Museum of Discovery in Little Rock, AR for verifying the accuracy of the information in this book.

Library of Congress Cataloging-in-Publication Data

Names: Kurtz, Kevin, author.
Title: Living things and nonliving things / by Kevin Kurtz.
Description: Mt. Pleasant, SC : Arbordale Publishing, [2017] | Series: Compare and contrast book | Audience: K to grade 3.
Identifiers: LCCN 2017018953 (print) | LCCN 2017024104 (ebook) | ISBN 9781628559880 (English Downloadable eBook) | ISBN 9781628559903 (English Interactive Dual-Language eBook) | ISBN 9781628559897 (Spanish Downloadable eBook) | ISBN 9781628559910 (Spanish Interactive Dual-Language eBook) | ISBN 9781628559859 (english hardcover) | ISBN 9781628559866 (english pbk.) | ISBN 9781628559873 (spanish pbk.)
Subjects: LCSH: Life (Biology)--Juvenile literature. | Organisms--Juvenile literature.
Classification: LCC QH309.2 (ebook) | LCC QH309.2 .K87 2017 (print) | DDC 570--dc23
LC record available at https://lccn.loc.gov/2017018953

Translated into Spanish: *Seres vivos y no vivos: Un libro de comparación y contraste*
Also available in these languages:
Arabic: الأشياء الحية والأشياء الغير حية: كتاب مقارنة وتباين PB ISBN 978-1-64351-4376
German: *Lebende Dinge und nicht lebende En Vergleichs- und Kontrastbuch* PB ISBN 978-1-64351-4772
French: *Le Vivant et le Non Vivant Points communs et différences* PB ISBN 978-1-64351-6011
Indonesian: *BENDA HIDUP dan BENDA TAK HIDUP* PB ISBN 978-1-64351-3775
Portuguese: *Seres Animados e Inanimados* PB ISBN 978-1-64351-4178
Japanese: 生物 と無生 物 PB ISBN 978-1-64351-3355
Mandarin Chinese *生物与非生物: 比较与对照手册* PB ISBN 978-1-64351-5403

English Lexile® Level: AD470L
key phrases: living, nonliving, compare and contrast, critical thinking

Printed in the US
This product conforms to CPSIA 2008

Arbordale Publishing
Mt. Pleasant, SC 29464
www.ArbordalePublishing.com